PAST IN PICTURES

A photographic view of
Hospitals

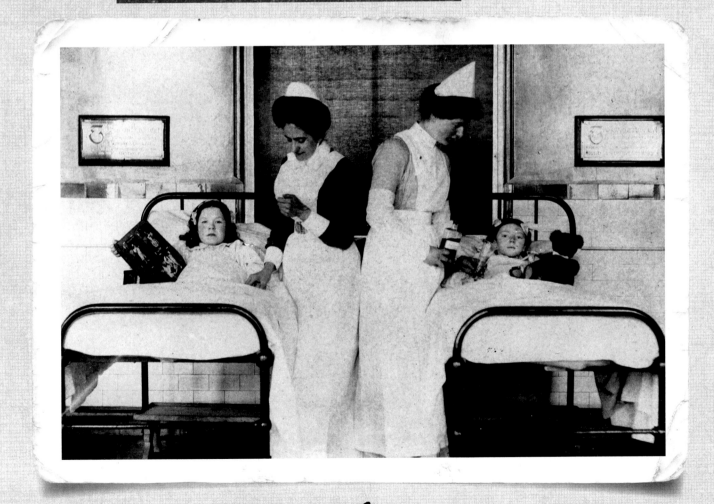

First published in paperback in 2015
Copyright © Wayland 2015

Wayland, an imprint of Hachette Children's Group
Part of Hodder & Stoughton
Carmelite House, 50 Victoria Embankment
London EC4Y 0DZ

Editor: Joyce Bentley
Concept Design: Lisa Peacock
Designer: Elaine Wilkinson
Researchers: Laura Simpson and Hester Vaizey
at The National Archives

Picture acknowledgements:
Material reproduced by courtesy of The National Archives, London, England. www.nationalarchives.gov.uk. Catalogue references and picture credits Main cover: COPY1/428 Guys Hospital London Child's bed 1897, COPY1/428 Guys Hospital London Nurse at bedside 1897, COPY1/511/165 Nurse Ashby holding the Murcott quadruplets from Long Eaton, 1907, COPY1/555/126 Beds in Children's Ward in Ashton Under Lyne District Hospital, 1911, Back cover: MH134/6 National Health Services midwife 1948-1957 title page: COPY1/555/126 Children's Ward in Ashton Under Lyne District Hospital, 1911, p2: INF2/43/2150 Afternoon tea, a British voluntary hospital 1944, p3: COPY1/547 Operating Theatre Great Northern Central Hospital Islington 1910, p4: ZPER34/59 p345 Hampstead Smallpox Hospital ward 1871, p5: COPY1/428 Guys Hospital London Child's bed 1897, p6: COPY1/428 Guys Hospital London Marys ward 1897, p7: COPY1/428 Guys Hospital London Nurse at bedside 1897, p8: COPY1/428 Guys Hospital London Miriam ward 1897, p9: COPY1/428 Guys Hospital London Operating Theatre 1897, p10: COPY1/428 Guys Hospital London Front surgery 1897, p11: COPY1/511/165 Nurse Ashby holding the Murcott quadruplets from Long Eaton, 1907, p12: COPY1/522/52 West London Hospital 1908, p13: COPY1/281 f384 Nurse's apron 'The Grace' 1909, COPY1/281 f382 Nurse's cap 'Dora' 1909, COPY1/281 f387 Nurse's cap 'St Ives' 1909, COPY1/281 f381 Nurse's cap 'Army' 1909, COPY1/281 f388 Nurse's apron 'The Rena' 1909, p14: COPY1/547 Circular Hospital Ward Great Northern Central Hospital Islington 1910, p15: COPY1/547 Operating Theatre Great Northern Central Hospital Islington 1910, p16: COPY1/555/126 Beds in Children's Ward in Ashton Under Lyne District Hospital, 1911, p17: COPY1/555/126 Children's Ward in Ashton Under Lyne District Hospital, 1911, p18: COPY1/555/126 Women's Ward in Ashton Under Lyne District Hospital, 1911, p19: Mary Evans Picture Library, p20: INF2/43/1169 Patients recuperate outdoors at RAF hospital 1943, p21: INF2/43/2150 Afternoon tea, a British voluntary hospital 1944, p22: INF2/44/2301 Breast cancer operation, 1944, p23: INF13/118/21 Train To Be A Nurse, p24: MH134/6 National Health Services nurse 1948-1957, p25: MH134/6 National Health Services ambulance medical equipment 1948-1957, p26: MH134/6 National Health Services midwife 1948-1957, p27: Mary Evans/Classic Stock/H. Armstrong Roberts, p28: Mary Evans Picture Library, p29: INF13/238/16 Recruitment of Nurses 1964-1973

Dewey number: 362.1'1

ISBN: 978 0 7502 8354 0

Printed in China

An Hachette UK company.

www.hachette.co.uk

www.hachettechildrens.co.uk

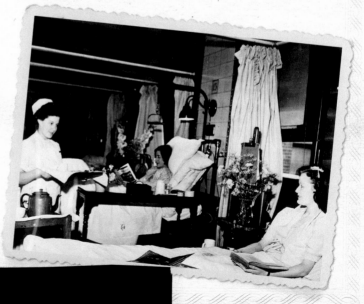

Contents

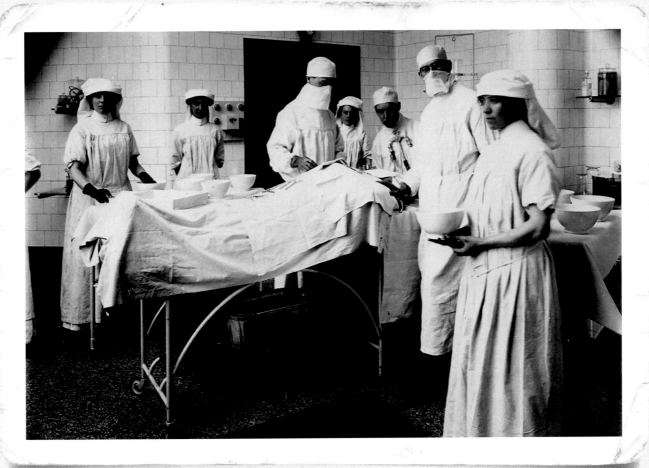

Introduction

In this book we look at photographs, as well as some other kinds of images of hospitals, from Victorian times up until the 1970s. We examine these images for clues about the past and see what we can learn from them about the way people used to live. On pages 30–31, you can find some questions and points to explore, to encourage further discussion of the pictures.

1871

← The people in this ward are suffering from smallpox.

↑ The nurses in this hospital ward are looking after people with smallpox. This infectious disease caused blisters on the skin and killed many people. Vaccination campaigns in the 19th and 20th centuries helped to eradicate smallpox.

1897

→ This is a ward for young children.

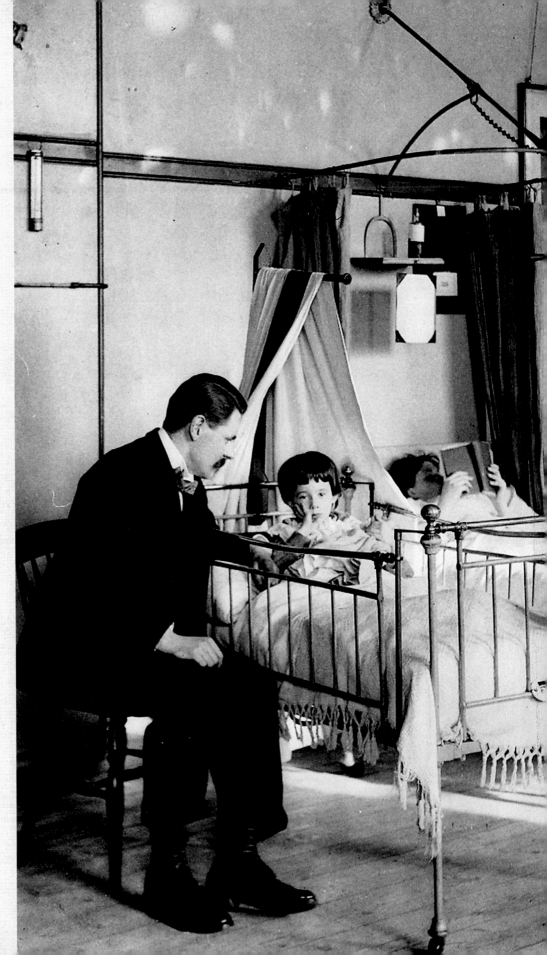

→ The first hospital beds with adjustable side rails appeared between 1815 and 1825. The wheels on the bed allow it to be moved about. For safety, the wheels are lockable.

↓ This is a ward for female patients.

↑ In this peaceful scene, nurses are checking on their patients or placing flowers by their bedside. In earlier eras, hospital wards were often dark, poorly ventilated and dirty. Conditions improved from the 1850s. Wards were regularly cleaned and large windows let in plenty of fresh air and daylight.

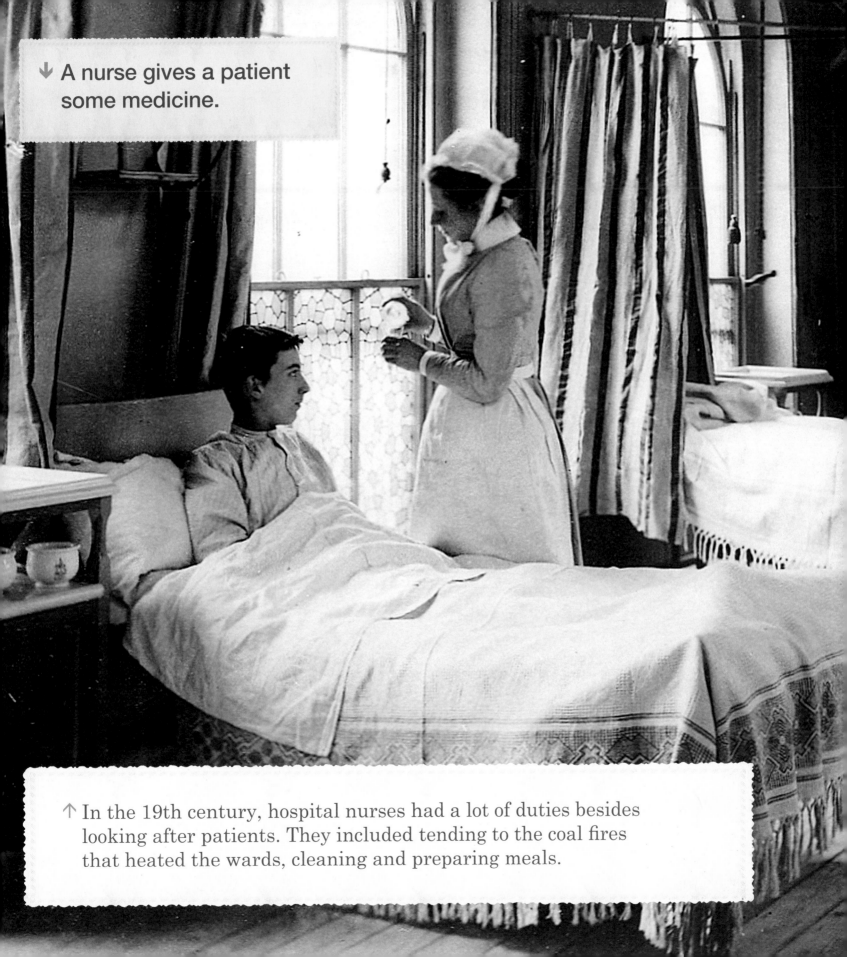

↓ A nurse gives a patient some medicine.

↑ In the 19th century, hospital nurses had a lot of duties besides looking after patients. They included tending to the coal fires that heated the wards, cleaning and preparing meals.

This is a ward in a children's hospital.

The first children's hospital in Britain was Great Ormond Street Hospital in London, which opened in 1852. Before then, children were placed on adult wards and were looked after by doctors with no training in children's health. This is Miriam's Ward in the Evelina Hospital for Sick Children, founded in 1869.

↓ A surgeon is operating on a patient.

↑ In the late 19th century, surgeons began to be aware of the importance of cleanliness in order to avoid infecting patients with germs. However, they continued to wear their own clothes to operate in until well into the 20th century.

↓ A surgeon treats an injured man.

↑ The casualty department of Guy's Hospital in London was known as the 'Front Surgery'. Here, people with minor injuries would wait in line to be treated by a surgeon. Unlike today, the procedure would often be carried out in front of other patients, rather than in a separate room.

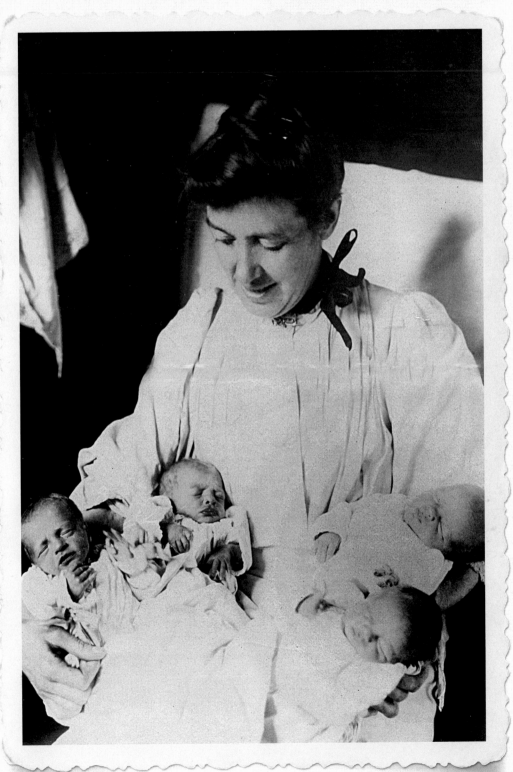

← A nurse holds a set of quadruplets.

← In the early 1900s, most births took place at home, attended by midwives. Maternity wards, where women could have their babies in hospital, became increasingly common during the 1920s and 1930s.

1908

↓ An injured man is being carried into a hospital.

↑ A man with a head injury is being carried on a stretcher into a hospital.
The man was probably brought to hospital in an ambulance. Unlike today,
ambulance drivers and stretcher bearers had little or no medical training.

⬇ Here are some drawings of some different kinds of nurse's cap.

Dora

St Ives

Army

The Grace

The Rena

↑ The nurse's cap was originally based on a nun's habit, as many of the earliest nurses were nuns. By the early 20th century there were many designs of nurse's cap, each with a different name. The frillier the design, the more senior the nurse.

⬇ **The ward of this hospital has a circular shape.**

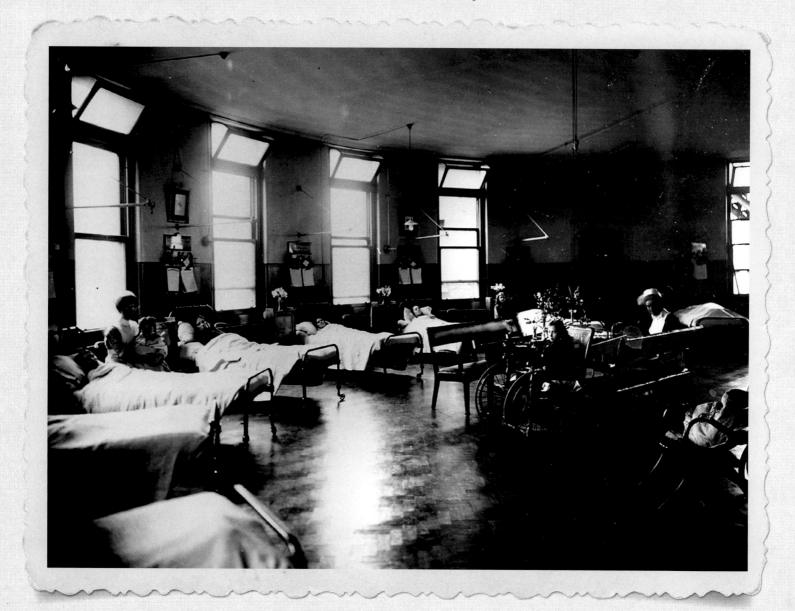

↑ This ward differs from the traditional rectangular design. The beds
have metal frames with wheels to make them easier to move around.
The little girl on the right is using an early example of a wheelchair
with spoked wheels.

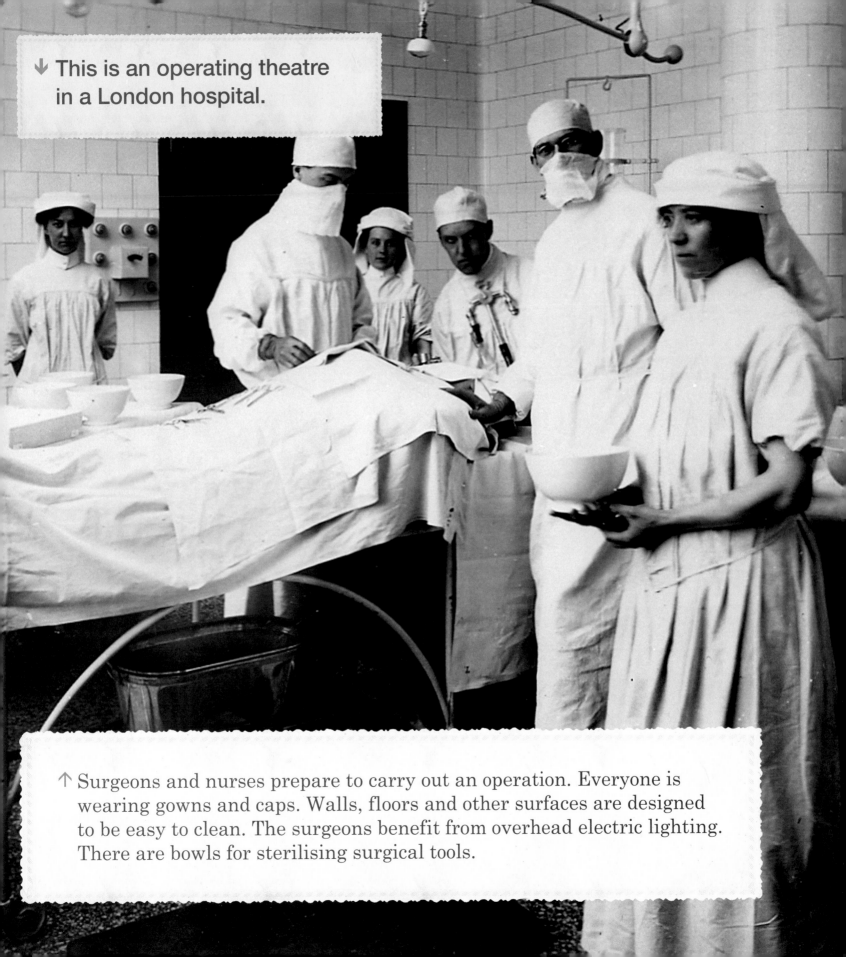

This is an operating theatre in a London hospital.

↑ Surgeons and nurses prepare to carry out an operation. Everyone is wearing gowns and caps. Walls, floors and other surfaces are designed to be easy to clean. The surgeons benefit from overhead electric lighting. There are bowls for sterilising surgical tools.

1911

↓ **This is a children's ward in a hospital.**

↑ This hospital ward is dedicated to caring for sick children, from infants to teenagers. It was not until 1922 that hospitals placed unwell newborn babies in a separate area, now called a neonatal intensive care unit.

↓ These little girls are being attended to by nurses.

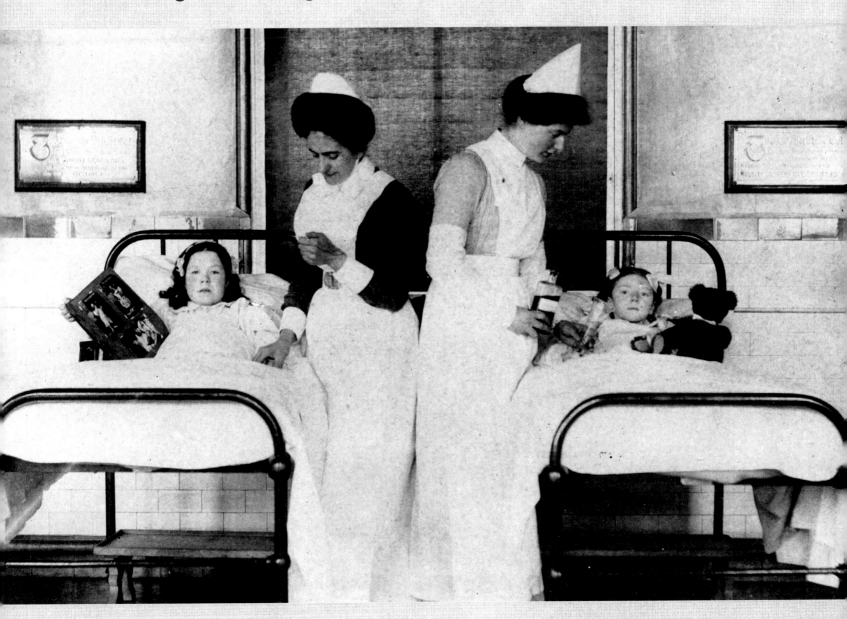

↑ The nurse on the left is checking her patient's pulse. The one on the right is offering the girl her medicine. The girls seem calm, but not very cheerful. Under their beds are wooden trays.

⬇ **This is the women's ward of a hospital.**

↑ This photograph shows a group of nurses standing at the ready by the patients' beds. The lady in the dark uniform is a senior nurse called a matron. She was in charge of all the nurses and was responsible for the efficient running of the hospital.

1930s

↓ **These hospital nurses are learning about human anatomy.**

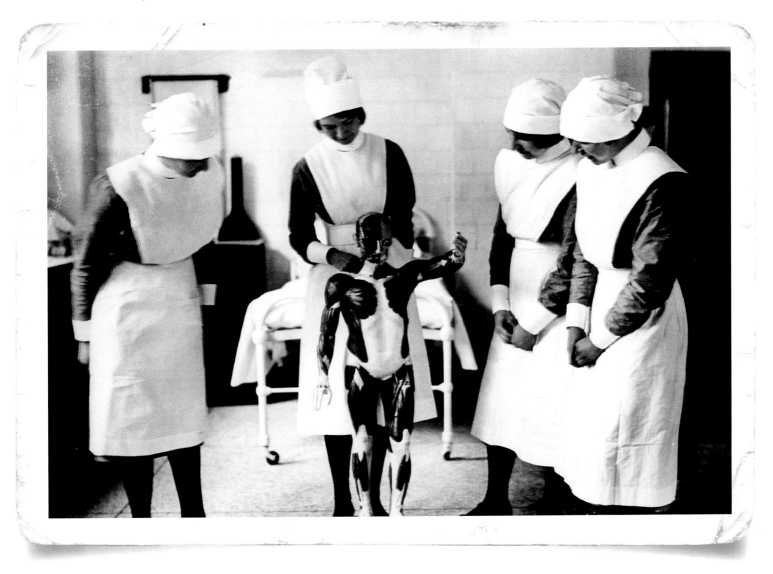

↑ These nurses are studying a model of the human body in order to learn about its different parts. In the 1930s, a nurse's training included anatomy, physiology (how the body works), patient care, first aid and the study of germs and disease.

↓ These RAF pilots are recovering from their injuries.

↑ During World War II, hospitals were set up to treat Royal Air Force (RAF) pilots injured in battle. The RAF had its own nursing service. In 1943, there were 1,126 RAF nurses, staffing 31 RAF hospitals and 71 station sick quarters. RAF nurses were often posted abroad to wherever battles were being fought.

↓ A nurse serves afternoon tea to the patients.

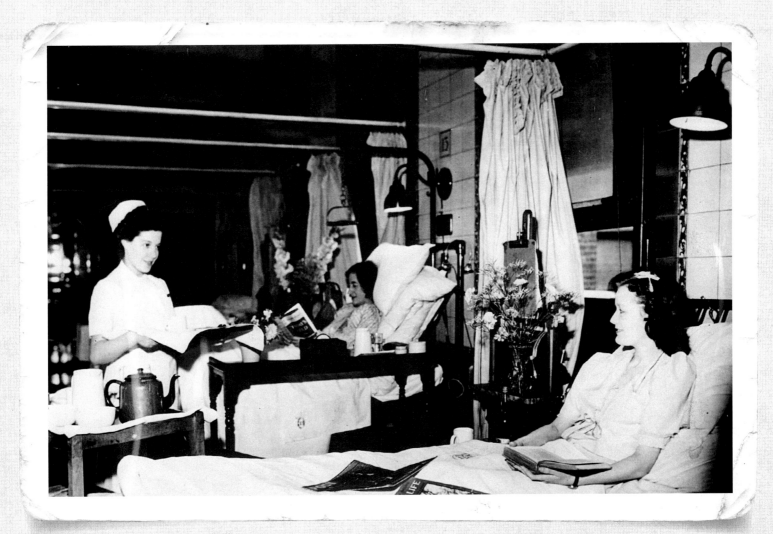

↑ This is a ward in a voluntary hospital. These were independent hospitals, paid for by charitable donations. But the hospitals were often short of money and beds. In 1948, the National Health Service (NHS) was founded. The government took over the voluntary hospitals. From then on, the hospitals were paid for by taxes and free health care was provided to all.

⬇ **These surgeons are operating on a patient.**

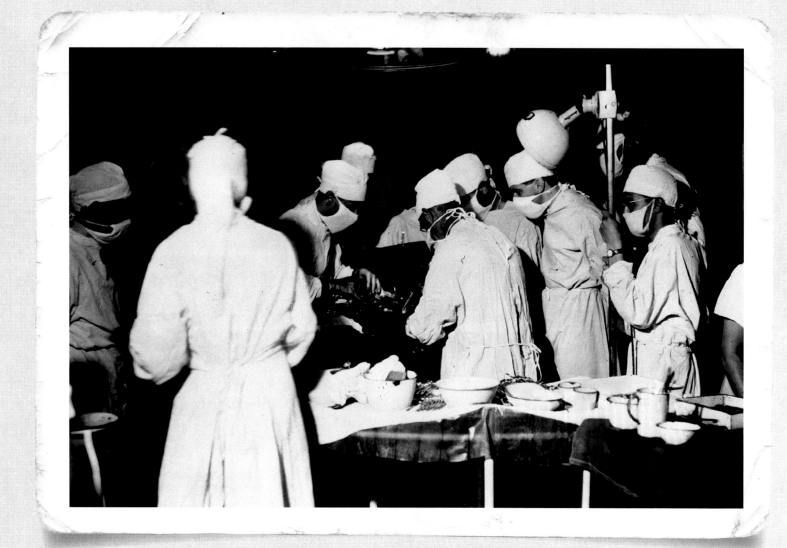

↑ Before the 1940s, surgery was dangerous because many patients died from infection and blood loss. The development of antibiotics and safe blood transfusion in the early 1940s made surgery a lot safer.

TRAIN TO BE A

NURSE

...A DISTINGUISHED CAREER

CLIXBY

← This poster is encouraging women to become nurses.

← During the 1940s, there was a shortage of nurses. This was partly because nurses were poorly paid and conditions were tough. Also, nursing was seen as a female job, and married women were discouraged from going out to work. This limited the pool of potential nurses.

↓ This is a district nurse. She is taking care of a patient in the lady's own home.

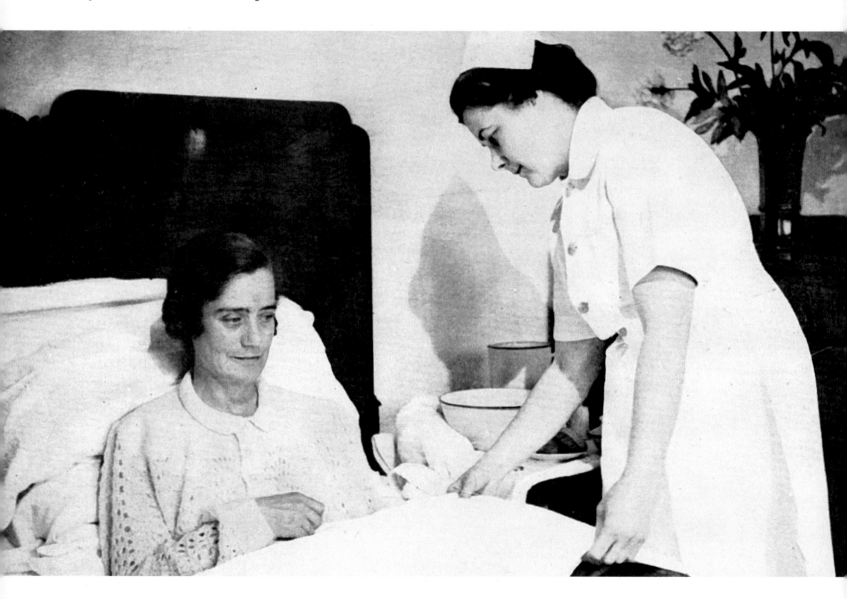

↑ District nursing began in the 19th century. District nurses work in their local community, rather than in a hospital. They visit house-bound patients and give them advice and medical treatment.

↓ These medical workers are helping a patient.

↑ Paramedics give emergency medical help to accident victims, to keep them alive until they can get them to hospital. This posed photo demonstrates some of their equipment. The paramedics are pretending to give an unconscious victim oxygen and tipping his body so that blood flows to his brain.

1948-57

→ A midwife watches a young mother bath her baby.

→ For centuries, midwives have assisted pregnant women and helped to deliver their babies. Traditionally, midwives learned their skills as apprentices but in the 1930s, formal training programmes were set up. Midwives can be male or female.

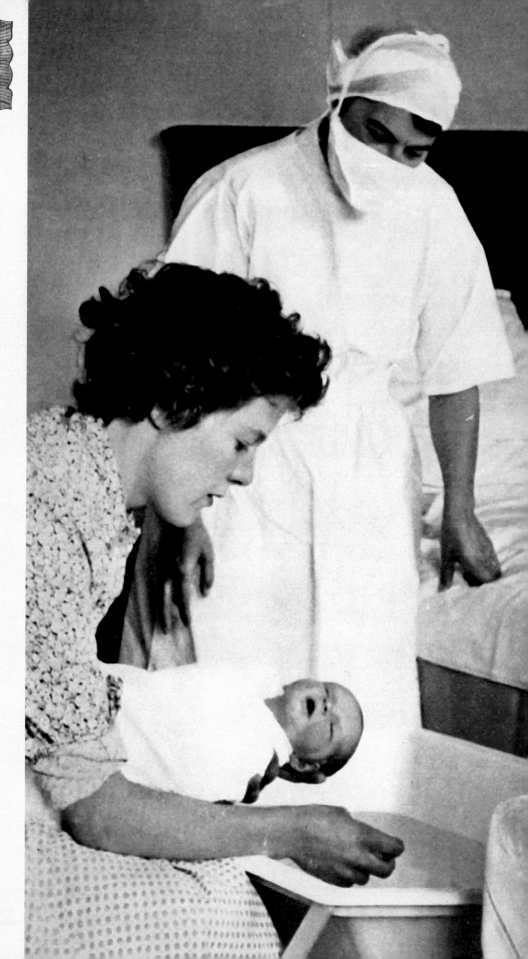

1960s

⬇ **A nurse feeds a premature baby in an incubator.**

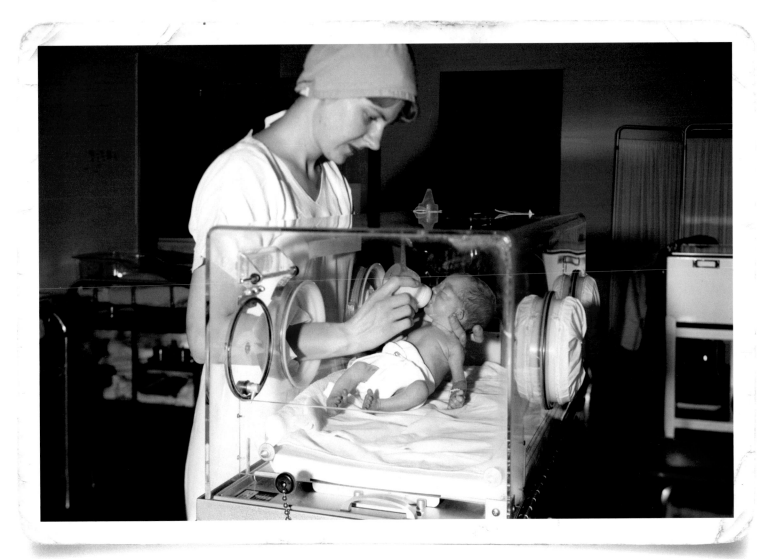

⬆ Some babies are born prematurely. They are placed in a device called an incubator to protect them from germs. The first incubators were invented in the late 19th century, but they only became common in hospitals during the 1950s and 1960s.

1968

↓ A patient receives radiation treatment for cancer.

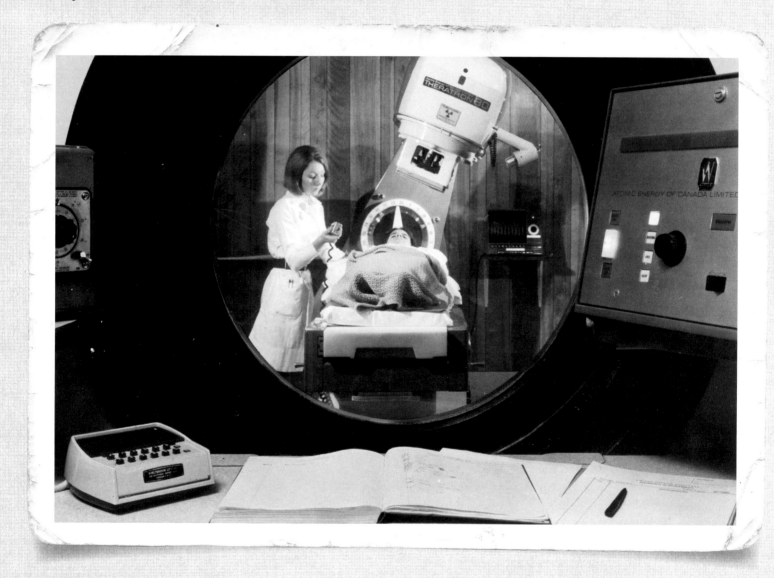

↑ In the 1930s, scientists discovered that a certain kind of radiation, or energy wave, could destroy cancer cells. During the 1950s and 1960s, radiation therapy machines began to appear in many hospitals to help treat people with cancer.

so many ways to help

Make a Career in the Hospital & Health Services.

← This poster is trying to encourage people to become healthcare workers.

← This poster shows some of the many jobs that people do in hospitals. It shows staff caring for patients, handling technical equipment, discussing diagnoses and preparing meals.

Questions to Ask and Points to Explore

Picture on page 4

Questions to ask

1. Does this seem like a comfortable environment for the patients? Give reasons.

2. Do you think these nurses might be at risk of catching smallpox from the patients?

3. Do some research into the disease and find out why they might be safe.

Points to explore

Room: size, light, windows, atmosphere, furniture

People: number, gender, clothes, pose, mood

Photograph on page 5

Questions to ask

1. There is a bottle on the shelf in the background., what do you think it contains?

2. Why do you think the cot is on wheels?

Points to explore

Room: furniture, bedclothes, decoration, equipment

People: age, clothing, mood

Photograph on page 6

Questions to ask

1. How does this scene differ from a modern hospital ward?

2. What is the same about it?

3. Why is there a jug and bowl on the left-hand side of the picture?

Points to explore

Room: furniture, decoration, plants and flowers, windows, lighting

People: gender, clothing, uniforms

Photograph on page 7

Questions to ask

1. How does this hospital bed differ from modern ones?

2. Does this photo look like real life, or do you think it might be posed?

3. For what reasons might this photo have been taken?

Points to explore

Room: furniture, décor, bedclothes, floor, window

People: gender, clothing, uniform

Photograph on page 8

Questions to ask

1. Why do you think there is a fireplace in the middle of the room?

2. Do you think this would be an enjoyable environment for children?

Points to explore

Room: space, light, windows, furnishings, table and bed coverings, plants

People: gender, age, clothing, uniforms

Photograph on page 9

Questions to ask

1. How does this scene differ from a modern operating theatre?

2. The patient has been laid on an ordinary table without wheels. Why might this be a problem?

3. What is the light for above the operating table?

Points to explore

Background: furniture, equipment, table coverings

People: gender, clothing

Photograph on page 10

Questions to ask

1. What might the dangers be of carrying out surgery in this way?

2. How many injured people can you see in this picture?

3. What are their injuries?

Points to explore

Room: decoration, furniture, lighting, fireplace, equipment

People: clothing, gender, age

Photograph on page 11

Questions to ask

1. Why do you think the nurse might be holding these newborn babies, and not the mother?

2. Between 1900 and 1930, infant mortality in Britain dropped from 140 to 63 deaths per thousand births. Why do you think that might be?

Points to explore

Person: gender, clothing, mood

Photograph on page 12

Questions to ask

1. Is the hospital entrance well designed for receiving accident victims? Can you think of any improvements that could be made?

2. Today, ambulance drivers and their attendants are trained in emergency medical care. What are these people called?

3. Can you see the name of this hospital?

4. Do some research on it and find out if it still exists.

Points to explore

Background: building, materials, windows, lighting

People: clothing, uniforms, gender, jobs, mood, urgency

Picture on page 13

Questions to ask

1. Do these nurse's caps look practical?

2. What might have been the advantages and disadvantages of wearing these caps?

3. How do these uniforms and caps differ from those worn by modern nurses?

Points to explore

People: gender, uniform

Art: style, depiction of women, intention

Photograph on page 14

Questions to ask

1. What might the advantages of a circular ward be, compared to a rectangular one?

2. In what other ways does this ward and its furnishing differ from those shown on previous pages?

3. This hospital has recently installed electric lighting. Apart from lighting, what other ways might a hospital benefit from electric power?

Points to explore

Room: shape, furniture, materials, windows, flowers

People: age, gender, uniforms, mood

Photograph on page 15

Questions to ask

1. Compare this photograph to the one on page 9. In what ways have operating theatres changed?

2. Does this look like a photo of a real operation? If not, why not?

3. What do you think the purpose of the photo might be?

Points to explore

Room: décor, materials, walls, floor, furniture, equipment, cleanliness, functionality

People: gender, uniforms, poses

Photograph on page 16

Questions to ask

1. How does this children's ward compare to the one on page 8?

2. How does it compare to modern hospital wards?

3. Does this look like a cheerful environment for children?

Points to explore

Room: size, number of beds, style of furniture, materials. plants, toys

People: age, gender, uniforms, clothes

Photograph on page 17

Questions to ask

1. What do you think the wooden trays under the bed might be used for?

2. One of the girls has a book; the other one has a teddy bear. If you had to spend time in hospital, how would you entertain yourself?

Points to explore

Room: materials, decoration, functionality, cleanliness

People: gender, uniforms, hairstyles, mood

Photograph on page 18

Questions to ask

1. How does the trolley on the right differ from modern trolleys?

2. What do you think might be in the bucket at the far end of the room?

Points to explore

Room: size, lighting, furniture, plants

People: gender, age, uniforms, pose

Photograph on page 19

Questions to ask

1. What might be the disadvantages of studying anatomy from a model?

2. What other ways can the human body be studied?

3. List their advantages and disadvantages.

Points to explore

Room: wall, floor, bed

People: gender, uniform

Photograph on page 20

Questions to ask

1. Can you tell what sort of injuries these young men are suffering from?

2. Why do you think they might be looking cheerful?

Points to explore

Background: beds, wheelchairs, crutches, screens, outdoor environment

People: age, gender, uniforms, clothing, injuries, mood

Photograph on page 21

Questions to ask

1. How does this scene differ from the one on page 20?

2. Do you think this scene is natural or posed? Why?

Points to explore

Room: furniture, tea things, flowers, curtains, décor

People: gender, uniform, clothing, hairstyles, expressions

Photograph on page 22

Questions to ask

1. Why are the surgeons wearing face masks?

2. How does this operating theatre differ from those on pages 9 and 15?

Points to explore

Room: equipment, lighting, furniture

People: number, gender, clothing

Picture on page 23

Questions to ask

1. Who is the shadow supposed to remind people of, and why is she holding a lamp?

2. What is this poster trying to say to people?

3. Does it get its message across clearly?

Points to explore

Art: style, depiction of women, text, typeface, intention

Photograph on page 24

Questions to ask

1. What are the advantages of providing care for patients in their homes rather than in a hospital?

2. Can you think of any disadvantages?

Points to explore

Room: furniture, bowl

People: gender, age, uniform

Photograph on page 25

Questions to ask

1. How does the ambulance in the background differ from modern ambulances?

2. What do you think the purpose of this posed photo is?

Points to explore

Background: vehicle, equipment, buildings

People: age, gender, uniforms

Photograph on page 26

Questions to ask

1. Why is the midwife wearing a gown and mask?

2. What other jobs do midwives do?

Points to explore

Background: bed, equipment

People: gender, clothing

Photograph on page 27

Questions to ask

1. Apart from keeping the baby isolated from germs, why else do you think incubators are useful?

2. This premature infant is being looked after on a general hospital ward. How do you think this differs from the way they are cared for today?

Points to explore

Room: equipment, furnishings

People: gender, uniform, headgear

Photograph on page 28

Questions to ask

1. The patient receiving radiation therapy is being photographed through a safety window. Any idea why?

2. The kind of radiation being used here is called ionising radiation. See what you can find out about it, and that should give you a big clue to Question 1.

3. We can see a pen and paper on the desk in front of the viewing window. What would you expect to see there today?

Points to explore

Room: equipment, window, bed

People: gender, uniform

Picture on page 29

Questions to ask

1. What is this poster trying to say to people?

2. Does it get its message across clearly?

3. Is it more or less effective than the poster on page 23?

4. Compare the depiction of the women in this poster with earlier photos in this book. How has it changed?

Points to explore

Poster: design, typeface, intention

People: gender, clothing, uniforms

Some suggested answers can be found on the Wayland website www.waylandbooks.co.uk.

Further Information

Books

Bedpans, Blood and Bandages: A History of Hospitals *(Raintree Freestyle: A Painful History of Medicine)* by John Townsend (Raintree, 2005)

Medicine in the Twentieth Century *(The History of Medicine)* by Alex Woolf (Wayland, 2006)

Public Health *(History of Issues)* by Adriane Ruggiero and Dawn Laney (Greenhaven Press, 2007)

Surgery *(Innovation in Medicine)* by Judy Alter (Cherry Lake, 2008)

Websites

http://www.gosh.nhs.uk/about-us/our-history/what-nursing-was-like/

http://www.hospitalsdatabase.lshtm.ac.uk/the-voluntary-hospitals-in-history.php

http://www.medicinethroughtime.co.uk

http://www.nmc-uk.org/About-us/The-history-of-nursing-and-midwifery-regulation/

http://www.nationalarchives.gov.uk/education/

Glossary

adjustable Able to be adjusted (altered or moved).

apprentice A person learning a trade from someone more experienced.

charitable donation A gift of money for a good cause.

diagnosis What is wrong with a person.

eradicate Get rid of.

infectious Likely to be passed on to other people or animals.

maternity ward A room in a hospital for women who are about to give birth, or who have recently given birth.

midwife A person (typically a woman) who assists women in childbirth.

neonatal Newborn.

nun's habit A long, loose garment worn by nuns.

operating theatre A room in a hospital where surgical operations are carried out.

paramedic A person trained in emergency health care.

pulse The rhythmic throbbing of the arteries as the heart pushes blood through them.

quadruplets Four children born at one birth.

Royal Air Force (RAF) The air force of the British Armed Forces, founded in 1918.

smallpox An infectious disease whose victims suffered fever and blisters on the skin, usually leaving permanent scars.

spoked wheels Wheels with wire rods connecting the centre to the outer edge.

sterilise To make something free of germs.

surgeon A person who is qualified to practise surgery.

surgery The treatment of injuries or illnesses with operations.

vaccination Treat with a substance that helps to make the body immune to a disease.

ventilate To allow air to circulate freely in a room.

ward A separate room in a hospital, usually provided for a particular type of patient.